AMONG THE
DOG EATERS

AMONG THE DOG EATERS

poems by

ADRIAN C. LOUIS

West End Press: Albuquerque

Some of the poems in this collection, a few in earlier versions, have appeared in *Chicago Review, Red Dirt, The Kenyon Review, The Greenfield Review, The Guadalupe Review, Contact II, Blue Cloud Quarterly, Studies in American Indian Literature, Circle of Motion, Coffeehouse Poets Quarterly, Mildred, Prairie Winds, Chiron Review, Blue Mesa Review, Zeitgeist, The Hawaii Pacific Review, Lactuca, Owen Wister Review, Birmingham Poetry Review, Pemmican, Black River Review,* and *The Nebraska Review.*

The author would like to thank Sally Dixon and the Bush Foundation of St. Paul, Minnesota for their generous fellowship grant which allowed the time to complete this book as well as other projects.

First Edition—June 1992
ISBN—0-931122-69-4

Cover photograph by Ron "Beef" Randall
Photo of author by Ricardo Block

West End Press
Box 27334
Albuquerque, New Mexico 87125

TABLE OF CONTENTS

Part One: *Among The Dog Eaters*

Part Two: *Unholy Redemptions*

Part Three: *Tombstones*

Part Four: *Coyote Songs*

Part Five: *Postscripts*

For all my relations,
living and dying.
To friends lost and found,
to drunks seeking sanity,
and especially to Colleen,
I dedicate this book.

*I thought about a meadow with flowers
at the end of the road, and I found a swamp.*
—Mariano Azuela

FOREWORD
by Jimmy Santiago Baca

Among The Dog Eaters, this new collection of poems by Adrian Louis, takes some very exciting and interesting risks. I first read the manuscript in Los Angeles, and now four months later, at Black Mesa, in New Mexico, I read it again. I had to let these poems simmer in me for that time. Anything real and potent takes time to work its way into the dream-land of our heart, a process that makes our life real.

Adrian Louis blows on the ashes and ignites the cinders of language. The importance of fire in language is equally as important as our use of fire in winter. He creates firelight by aiming the word closer and closer to the heart, where the blood pounds and feeds our arteries with life.

But it is more than that. He carves language to contain experience that is hard to grasp and tell about. He deals with margin-life, the blood and betrayals, the bleak joys and raging ecstasies of our lonely, primal dance as humans living in a world insanely intoxicated on cheap thrills.

Ultimately, our lives are either truthful journeys or philandering lies, whiskey-eyed tales made up of half-truths to bolster our weakling attempts at living honorable lives. And these poems in *Among The Dog Eaters* are the clothing of a man slowly stripping himself naked before the powers of the earth and sky and allowing us to hear the song of the poet on a journey into the darkness to create light out of the sheer love of language. Poetry is the flute that Louis plays, and with that flute he brings order to anarchy and confusion. The light that he creates brightens a dark, harsh world with simple and unwavering truth.

The language stands upright, in our faces, and fights, surrenders, challenges—and ultimately we hear the voice of a poet who has come home again and sings in his dark room, happy that his voice is his again. And, thousands of miles way, his magic is carried on the wind. His voice here on these pages affirms my belief that good poems are like the legs of a man or woman, carrying that individual up a hard climb to discover the secrets of the heart. And those are the secrets that we all need to know to live better lives and write with the strength of stones, full of infinite silence that is the essence of the first spark of creativity.

These poems force experience to unveil its face. It seems in many of the poems as if Louis manages to call the spirits back from the other side to this side, and the voices of the spirits seem to talk to us. It is not only the voice of the poems but the images that startle one with their physical and evanescent presence. It is as if this book is a long prairie with tall grass reaching to the horizon. One suspects that no one lives out there, that no one could possibly be out there, yet if you keep your eyes long enough on the swaying grass, a man rises and starts toward you, speaking poems. They leave you in wonder and wondering, asking so many questions about life. That is what they have done to me.

—Black Mesa (Albuquerque, N.M.)
October 1991

PART ONE:

AMONG THE DOG EATERS

NOTES FROM INDIAN COUNTRY

I am Odysseus, son of Laertes. All men take account of my wiles and my fame has reached high heaven. My home is in Ithaca, fair in the evening light.

—Homer, *The Odyssey*

An adjectival all-staff meeting at the Indian
college: useless and mandatory. Later
we were forced to listen to a *professional*
storyteller titter her version of odd Odysseus
returning to the horny climes of Ithaca.
She mimed stringing the bow of Eurytus but
the wide-eyed skins were asleep
except for Verdell
who let a silent onion fart.

Last week I told my Freshman English class
that one hundred years ago there was no
difference between the sentence
and the paragraph.
I can't recall where I gleaned that tidbit
or whether or not it was apocryphal.
Then I could not remember
why paragraphs should be
hinged by transitions.

This fixation carried me through the meeting
and took me to the dusky indifference
of Pine Ridge, fair in the evening light.
Home from work I grilled greasy green hamburger
from Sioux Nation Shopping Center.
The glowing coals and mosquitos took me away
from the wannabees, squawmen, and white liberals
who pretend to save Indians by daylight
but vacate the reservation when wild
redskin night rolls in.

With my pot gut and can of Bud I stood
holding my stainless steel spatula
on my neatly trimmed lawn,
the only one in Pine Ridge.

The rest of my neighbors, less crazy,
fill their yards with the flotsam
of American advertising: used Pampers, dead cars,
punctured tires, and empty beer cans
until buzzards swarm like flies
and carry away their unwatched children.

Looking at the seared meat, once sacred
I had a fleeting vision of hope
that eluded grasp.
I was contemplating democracy
and the Chinese students in Peking
who had been failed by America
and how American Indians were Asiatic
yet we are a people beyond definition.
We are not a sentence or a paragraph
and we are definitely
not stanzaic.

Another day at the Indian college was done
and so were my burgers so I moved
them from the grill
and carried the grease lumps
to my old lady who was looking grumpy,
slicing onions.

We lugged two K-Mart foldup chairs
into our Indian yard
and sat with our humble meal until I popped
the top on my fourth can of Bud.

Ain't even dark, she chastised but her eyes
were moved by something tumbling
from a diseased elm along the chainlink
fence we put up to protect the thieves and winos
from our ball-biting dogs.
I saw that it was one of our retarded cats falling
from a tree in an abortive dive at a swallow.
I told her it was a small child
just dropped by a passing turkey buzzard.
The bird of prey's talons had grasped the kid

by the temples, dropping him
brain-damaged back
onto Sioux Indian land.
This is your legacy, I said opening another beer
and she went inside without a word.
I threw my full beer at the cat
and concentrated on my burger.
I closed my eyes and dreamed of McDonald's.
Yes, I closed my eyes
and dreamed of McDonald's.

AFTER LONG SILENCE MARILYN RETURNS

I.

Another all-staff meeting at the Indian college
run by white UFO's who pull the strings
of visionless Indian administrators.
The crazy *wasicus* again are all present,
each having crawled out
from his own queer rock:
the Indian savers, the squawmen with hair grown long,
the culture vultures, the failed academics
who could not work elsewhere,
they're all here alongside the smaller number
of truly concerned white people
but they all make me so nervous
that I exit the meeting and run to the bathroom
to pick my nose and check my balls
which is when I remember you, my Paiute girl,
my Marilyn.

A long time ago my hands
were on you like the frantic fawnings
of unclaimed dogs in the pound
awaiting the deep-needle sleep.

II.

I plumbed the gossamer between Budweiser
and nose-pinching, face-slapping anxiety
so much it took me forty years to reach twenty-five.
Even now, *ennut*, the hot green of springtime
comes casting shadows
of concrete and fear on my heart.
The first time I kissed you the daffodils
throbbed as you breathed in the dark.

Now you come to me as semi-succubus
minus the histrionics of our history.
We were young and Indian and purer

than any whiteman school-learned philosophy
but now or maybe then
the deadly saltpeter of time
extinguished the smoldering sage of our love
leaving me here in this polysyllabic lunacy:
this perverse perpetuation
of the white man's paternalism.

III.

Some joker is talking about the financial stability
of our institution opposed to the fact
that our paychecks may be delayed,
but I think back to the time when I was recovering
after they tried to poison me with Jesus
and I chased sun-colored visions of love
with you into celluloid cauldrons where
amidst democratic and popcorn desires we kissed
and groped like the teenagers we were.

At about that time I would have driven
a uranium spike into Krushchev's skull
to win your love, Marilyn. . .

O Christ of the raggedy-ass old cross!
I am getting old; Russia is now our ally.
The years have flittered away
like calendar pages in an old B-movie.
You've been dead a good, long time.
You died from a long, good time:
cirrhosis at thirty.

IV.

Marilyn!
Romantics will not allow
that the darkness has an unwashed smell.
In the near hell of halfbreed childhood
I zig-zagged through the star-shy snow

in catalog shoes bought too big
dragging a branch behind.
No one would follow my path
to the half moon door.

Running against shame I was stopped
by a decrepit gelding work horse
spewing white breath at the heavens. I
screamed, wet my pants, and leaped to its back
and charged towards the future
with the false lance of intellect lightening
the darkness, Jesus
the darkness, Jesus
of our blood-drenched Indian land.

—Kyle, South Dakota
May 1989

THIS IS NO MOVIE OF NOBLE SAVAGES

Born of trees
whose timeless atoms
carried on their savage
act of indolence
in annual assault of leaves
upon the earth
while their branches
felt up the sky
where the white man's God lives,
this paper
holding these petroglyphs
is neither apology nor legacy
but a wanted poster.

Now, dauntless before Dante's
nocturnal emissions
of visions of Hell
I curse God and weep
because some creeps crept
through the back window and carried
away my typewriter
while we were at the wake.
When I find them,
they will bleed broken English
from shattered mouths
and my fists
will sing songs of forgiveness,
unless of course
they're my in-laws.

PALM SUNDAY IN PINE RIDGE

The inhabitants of the earth are of two sorts: Those with brains but no religion, and
those with religion but no brains.   —Abu al-Ma'arri

A furled leaf on a dying rubber plant
in our dull bedroom does penance
to uninformed roots.
This is high plains winter.

Like a green cigar it arches angrily
aching for the weak sun
flitting through ragged curtains
of Irish lace bought at K-Mart.

Above your dresser's fleet of jars
a hard-assed hardwood crucifix
beams so glibly that I rise wobbling
to touch the chest of Christ.

Dust and cat hair cover the wooden
redoubt of your convent years.
Your Jesus has lint in his belly button.
Such sights are not good for hangovers.

I flop back to bed and light a Marlboro.
I think briefly of igniting the leaf, but simply
blow smoke rings at the ceiling.
Outside the bully snow is pushing
drifts against our housing unit.

The spirit of Calvary brought by blackrobes
has placed us between two worlds.
This is Palm Sunday and you're at church.
I need strong coffee but I'll be damned
if I'll get up and make it.

A VISIT TO MY MOTHER'S GRAVE

Now twenty years old
my mother's tombstone looks brand-new.
I draw clean air,
count to ten and walk towards the west.
My skeletons have been burnished
golden they dance
in the crimson morning.

In a nearby alfalfa field
I stop to breathe
and watch some Paiute boys bucking
bales off the parched back
of their mother, the earth.

They break for lunch
in a small shack of corrugated tin.
I have walked from the graveyard
and into the hayfield
just to visit with them.
Through the rusted nail holes
in the sheet metal roof
puffs of light explode
like ladyfingers of God-glint
reflected and refracted on the brown boys' sweat
and I'm forced to sing
this mirage of rainbows
this mingled prayer
this visit to my mother's grave
this soil of Nevada
this soil of Wovoka
this song of love
for my people.

AT THE KNIGHT'S INN IN RENO

The rising sun
over casinos blinks
briefly honoring nothing
and then scurries daybreak tourists
on streets shyly Indian.
Local lurkers with long sideburns
and other cretins freed
by economic necessity
from the state nut house
flee from the impending
order of light.
Even winos
who lack clean underwear
do not like to see sanity
sprout like white
mold or watch
street-sweep trucks
grumbling in their beards.

In the Knight's Inn,
an Indian bar,
the brown eyes blink redly
at absenting night.
We sit listening to ancient Harry Belafonte
delivering "Day-O."
Daylight comes
and we want to go home
but our mother, the earth,
has been murdered
and we helped the white man
do the dirty deed.

RAIDING PARTY

We totter
creep forward
bagging tomatoes
tumescent cucumbers
big stalk carrots
with impotent roots.

Drunk, giggling
forty years old
raiding the neighbors' gardens
like we did
as young boys.

In one backyard
we see a woman undressing
inside her bedroom.
This is pure
Paiute madness.
You are my best friend.
You are my best friend
from Indian childhood.
Let's crawl on home
and finish the bottle.
My friend, my friend,
my best boyhood friend,
they have told me you're dying of cirrhosis.

CHRISTMAS CAROL FOR THE SEVERED HEAD OF MANGAS COLORADAS

One of the miners walking about the camp that night later testified: "About 9 o'clock I noticed the soldiers were doing something to Mangas. I discovered that they were heating their bayonets in the fire and burning his feet and legs. Mangas angrily protested that he was no child to be played with."

—Benjamin Capps, *The Great Chiefs*

I.

With eyes of dead fish
bloated on dreams of a white Christmas
Nordic sodbusters in polyester scourge Rushmore Mall
enforcing the sordid joy of the season.
More than anything I hate shopping for presents.
I do it because I love you,
because it's expected, a mandatory ritual
for the little girl in you who existed
before you prostrated yourself
before that alabastered Christ
of your convent years in Denver.
And it gives me a day away from the squalor,
the aimlessness of the reservation.

In Waldenbooks I buy a paperback
Webster's Collegiate Dictionary
to use as a stocking stuffer.
Two giddy airmen from Ellsworth AFB
behind me in the checkout line
snort and snicker and I know
it's because of my long ponytail.
It doesn't matter, I tell myself.
I'm too old to take offense.
Besides, I know I could rip out
both of their throats at the same time
if I had to. These ass-wipe airheads
of a television generation blather
proudly of recent air war weaponry.
"Woulda saved time, just to nuke

them towel-head sand niggers," one says.
I shake my head and bite my lip
so I won't ask them to strap me on for size.
Sweet Mother of God...
They're already trapped in the clownish blue
the flesh turns when deprived of air.

II.

Apocrypha: The bullet brain sleep of Mangas Coloradas.
In the dry American past
in the dry American Southwest
near a place called Pinos Altos
stink-butt redneck troopers
under the common command of Gen. Joseph R. West
captured the famous *Mimbres* chieftain
who had come to talk of peace.

Bluecoats dried his Apache dream of rain.
They roused him from sweet desert sleep
by applying heated bayonets to his feet
and laughed as they shot him four times,
then scalped him and chopped off his head.
Later, an Army surgeon removed
his savage brain and measured it somehow.
Scholars at the time were amused
and amazed that it measured
the same weight as Daniel Webster's.

I know better now.
It would have weighed much more.
It would have weighed an eternity of tears
and rage if one could imagine
an Apache warrior ever crying.
One tear of Mangas Coloradas would outweigh
all the Indian history books ever
written by white men.

III.

I pay for the dictionary
contrived by Webster's cousin Noah
and grow with each imagined word.
After pretending to window shop
I follow the two bluecoats
to the parking lot.
My fists are itching.
Christmas carols have been piped outside
and a dainty snow is falling.
Sometimes I have no common sense.
There are no words in the book for me.
My fists are itching and snow is whitening
when I turn and head for my car.
This is a time of peace. Christ,
how I hate your extended birthday party.
Christ, how I want to kick some ass,
just beat the piss out of flyboys.

DUST WORLD

for Sherman Alexie

I.

Whirlwinds of hot autumn dust
paint every foolish hope dirty.
I stand in the impudent ranks of the poor
and scream for the wind to abate.
Prayers to Jesus might be quicker
than these words from blistered hands
and liquor, but the death wind
breaks the lines to God.
I have no sylvan glades of dreams,
just dust words
for my people dying.

II.

With pupil-dilated *putti* in arms
three teenaged mothers
on the hood of a '70 Chevy
wave at me like they know me.
Inside the video rental
a small fan ripples sweat
and scatters ashes upon two young attendants
practicing karate kicks and ignoring me
because they're aware I could dust
their wise asses individually or collectively.
They're products of Pine Ridge High
which means they would have had two strikes
against them even if they did graduate
and these two clowns never did.
I guess they're almost courting me,
in a weird macho way almost flirting,
because I'm fatherly, half buzzed-up,
and have biceps as thick as their thighs.
Heyyyy. . .ever so softly,
this is the whiskey talking now.

III.

With pupils dilated and beer in hand
three teenaged mothers court frication
more serious than their sweet Sioux butts
buffing the hood of their hideous car.
When I glide my new T-bird
out of the video store parking lot
they wave like they really know me.
One of the girls, beautiful enough
to die for except for rotten teeth
smiles and I suck in my gut
and lay some rubber.
I cruise through a small whirlwind
of lascivious regrets
and float happily through the dark streets
of this sad, welfare world.

This is the land that time forgot.
Here is the Hell the white God gave us.
The wind from the Badlands brings
a chorus of chaos and makes everything dirty.
I meander past my house and stop briefly
before driving back to where
the young girls are.
I park my car and re-enter the store.
The two young boys are still dancing
like two cats in mid-air, snarling, clawless
and spitting. No harm done.
I stare them down and place two cassettes,
both rated X, on the counter.
It's Friday night and I'm forty years old
and the wild-night redskin
parade is beginning.

AMONG THE DOG EATERS

My *kola* from *Pejuta Haka* called
two weeks ago tuned tightly and fired up.
"It's the same on most reservations," he said.
"These white men come in
and steal our women . . .
They become Indians by insertion! Instant
experts on redskin culture. Once they dip their wicks
they start speaking of Indians as . . . *us*!
When Indian men spit upon these squawmen,
the squawmen lick the spit and get stiff dicks.
The result is novels by white poets who label
themselves *Native Americans,* anthropological
monographs by liberal assholes,
and more breeds like you."

Last week, when April in its fecund lunacy
brought skunks courting mates
to the finality of speeding cars,
some squawmen and skins across the reservation
organized a march against violence
but very few came.
It was a full moon and the entire population
was behaving like a one-legged man
in an ass-kicking contest.
Everybody was too busy beating
the shit out of each other.
Men were stabbing women.
Women were clubbing kids.

Yesterday, in Big Bat's Conoco Station,
I overhead a squawman whining
how he could not fathom
such limited response to salvation.
I dewaxed my ears and heard him clearly
saying they *were* brothers, weren't they?
The meek and mere fact of fathering Indian kids
had put them on the good, red road,
hadn't it?
What the hell is going on here, he asked his

white brother, and then they both lamented
the failure of their long march
across the Pampers-strewn reservation.
We wanted to help *the people*, he said
in the saddest of tones.
With *that*, I lost listening to his void
and went to the counter to order more coffee.

We wanted to help *the people*.
The People...ennut?
I added Sweet n' Low to my cup
and watched a small red ant
scurry across the white formica table.
We wanted to help *the people*.
The ant danced in circles around spilled sugar
imitating our Indian nations.
When white men come onto Indian land
and try to lead by forlorn example,
I want to laugh and cry at the same time.
If only they understood:
the savages don't want to be tamed!
We wanted to help *the people*...

I watched the formic creature stagger
around the white crystals,
intoxicated upon the largesse
of some alien God.
Once, in a time before body hair
I placed two red ants atop a lonely craft
made from a popsicle stick and sailed them
down a rain-swollen ditch
as if I myself, were a God.
We wanted to help *the people*...

There are so many things the white man
refuses to see, I thought as I crushed the ant.
By his naming us *victims*, we become victims.
When he says we are *oppressed*,
we learn to oppress each other.
But is he why we must accept welfare?
Is he why we drink and beat our wives?

Is he why we molest our children?
And is he why we are programmed to fail?

In Big Bat's Conoco I wanted to scream:
Wake up, you damn *people*, wake up!
America does not owe you a living.
America does not owe you your souls.
You've got to grab your balls
and fill them with fire
and stop whining
and drinking like bums,
but all I did was murder
an ant.

for Robert Gay

PETROGLYPHS AND OTHER VOICES

In an ancient cave halfway up
the sandstone cliffs
some elders you knew
said an evil, ancient renegade
had once been buried
until white settlers
removed his dusty bones
and scattered them in jest.

For some reason
I stared at your lovely Assiniboine ass
and thought you would understand
what my old lady could not.

We scurried up towards the cave,
two sweating academics
catching our breath
before entering a threshold
marked by irrational petroglyphs.
Was that a stick figure with a knife
standing beneath a flying eagle?
Something about it made my skin crawl
and held me from entering
the soft darkness of ghosts.

Let's get out of here, I said to you.
There's a bad feeling here.
Something is not right.
We backed away from the cave's entrance
and I stumbled and dropped my pack loaded
with camera and your papers and charcoal
for making rubbings of the ancient scrawl.
We had planned to burn sage
and offer a prayer
before we ascended but forgot to.

Down from the hill,
we gathered our senses at your four-wheel drive
and ate cold chicken and drank cold coffee

from my defective thermos.
A palpable power resided in the cave,
an evil spirit, we both agreed,
the ghost of a renegade who killed all races.

Finished eating, we regained strength
and lost purported foolishness.
We decided to climb to the cave again.
Panting from the dusty ascent,
we thought we heard whispers
above the wind.
In that bloodfire cave a sooted singer
decried the fire of our noon day womb.
I dropped my cigarette and held your hand.
We shook our heads wearily
and sloped down the hill, again.

The charred remains of animal night
ripped into dream vision and startled
our hearts like a light bulb to hand.
The evil spirit carried his soul
from the cave wall
into my mind.
The spirit warmed my flesh and congealed
my emotions with coldness.
I felt like throbbing meat meant
for the bloated starving.
I knew the renegade killed for pleasure.
I thought that when I reached for your breast.
We were not lovers.
Simply friends and co-workers.
We both blushed at my incongruous hand
and one minute later
it had never happened.

Late at night in bed
with my old lady sleeping, I thrashed
with thoughts of the bad spirit cave.
Something was thumping against my front
door, but it was only my dogs
returned from their dream.

There were no spirits there.
Any voices from that cave have long disappeared.
The petroglyphs remain unseen,
except for the whisper
of the ghost wind of words:
that renegade lives
in my dark cave of mind.

SUNSET AT PINE RIDGE AGENCY

Waiting for you waiting for foodstamps,
I watch an old man with a brown face
and swollen red nose
lower the flag
at the Pine Ridge Agency
and try to control it
against the frivolity
of a slapping wind.

The Medusan stripes are phallic
and seem to ejaculate
the yellowed stars
onto faded blue cloth.

Rouge smothers the sagging breasts
of these Indian hills
which hide the unmarked grave
of Crazy Horse.

In cubist shadows adjoining
the roseate patina
drunks stab and rape
(Is there a difference?)
other drunkards and nobody
gives a good God damn.

This Indian nation is in anarchy
dancing awkwardly toward the day
when it will fall off the edge
of the bed of the world
and awake to its own suicide.

IN THE GHETTO ON THE PRAIRIE
THERE IS UNREQUITED LOVE

In the imperfect prefecture
of stone and sky
the sauna breath of August
simmers commonplace dogs.
They circle paths through the sun
softened asphalt of Sioux
Nation Shopping Center
where stretched out in the shade
of the loading dock
winos bask and bake
in the luxuriant miasma
of slow death
and the only thing
separating me from them
is my growing need for you
and the fear that I might die unloved.

ELVIS PRESLEY IN PINE RIDGE

At the Pine Ridge Village Pow-wow
Verdell wobbles, hungover,
beneath the pine shades
and curses the ignorant kids,
halfbreeds and fullbloods
break-dancing to *Vanilla Ice*
on a boom box blasting ten yards
away from the Porcupine Singers.
Sweating, he watches a ravishing
young lady fancy dancer
kick up the clay dust
that clings to his wine sweat.
She spins like she owns the land!
Her spinning binds his heart
with desperate longing
and he sways into the recognition
of the fact that if he could have her,
his whole life would change,
things would be good,
he'd be young again
and his future would stand before him.

Lakota drums stop.
The *wacipi* ends, but the breakers
continue and Verdell watches
the teenaged fancy dancer,
ever dignified and not even sweating,
untangling a knot in her shawl.
She has danced him into exhaustion
with her hawk nose and thighs
so perfect he would
even pray to Jesus
just to jump
her fourteen year-old bones.

His lips curl defiantly
and his forty-one year-old balls
pout and pound in remembrance of youth.
He instantly wants to defend her honor

against the intrusive rap boom box
but he can't remember what honor
means these days.
Sometimes he thinks the only honor
remaining is to die upon Indian land.

Verdell would have laughed at the thought
of dying, when at her age, fourteen
he wore an Elvis pompador
and did the jitterbug in pegged jeans.
Through the dust of now and then
he smiles and turns his collar up.
Sneering, and tightening his stomach,
he mumbles softly,
"One for the money,
two for the show.
Three to get ready,
now go cat, go!"

THE SWEAT LODGE

The last round began
and the outside
world did not exist.

Black heat slammed
me to the ground and I kissed
the cool, cool earth.

The lead man was an old radical:
"You suffer to be a man"
was said unsaid.

Devil red rocks laughed
and pulled the booze
from my half-Paiute bones.

Angry spirits from the west
spit words which are best
left alone, unrepeated.

"Grandfather," I prayed.
"Let me live, *ennut*, I promise
I'll never touch a drop again."

Dancing lights of green and red
shot from my eyes and I sighed
when the flap was finally opened.

A week later I was at the Oasis Bar
in Rapid City drinking with Verdell
and countless forlorn urban skins.

It was air-conditioned there.
Jimi Hendrix was inside the jukebox
lost in the purple haze of time.

PART TWO:

UNHOLY REDEMPTIONS

THE HUNTER'S BLOOD QUICKENS

It has come to this: no booze
and no blood-red meat.
I shudder at the plate before me.
Boiled chicken stripped of skin
and vegetables blanched of taste.
I sip bubbles of diet Pepsi.

Last winter I
was drunk and pouted, snarling
as you handed me ribboned gifts
but it is late summer now.
The yellow pine needles on the dead
Christmas tree in the back yard
refuse to make more dry words
or fade the pages
of a faded life further.

The bleached bones of a Badlands steer
I rustled and butchered
on Indian land last fall
are scattered in my yard by my dogs.
It was a waning moon night
when I popped the .45
into the head of the "Slow Elk."
Verdell and I loaded the beast
in the back of my small Ford Escort wagon.
We were covered with blood
and ruined the upholstery.

A pile of empty booze bottles
slowly purpling in the field
an arm's reach beyond my back yard
reminds me of no guilt.
I only remember succulent T-bones,
plump-ass rump roasts,
and good, meaty ribs for my dogs.

AT A GRAVE IN AN EASTERN CITY

"There are those that break and bend. I'm the other kind."

—Steve Earle

I.

Oh, fuck me it's cold. Diamond-white
snow falls on my shivering shoulders
as I stand above the bones
of an American poet.

Time has rusted his symphony
but I recall the shouts
touting misbegotten angels
of worlds I yearned to see.
Their wings fanned and flamed
urges born on desolate Indian land
and beckoned me to roads
crisscrossing this carrion nation.

Elegy is such personal business.
I don't want to say what I mean
and I don't mean to say
what I want.
These very words, this moaning
between blue and true arises
as it once arose from the same old sad
something now throbbing between my thighs.
Christ, there is *always* the meticulous hint
of eggs, the fluid of which can't make
me chicken but still gets me again and again
to the other side of the bad joke street
where the preferred meat
is always white.

In a city not far from this one I passed
my early twenties as a white man
some twenty years ago.
Not a soul had seen me as a boy digging
the harsh soil of Northern Nevada

moving the outhouse
through the speeding seasons.
No one there had seen the dark brown face
of my mother.
And no one had seen the shack without water
that twelve of us kids grew up in.

II.

We gave them corn which, once popped
into miniature buttered clouds,
gave us the opportunity to watch ourselves:
bloodthirsty, slow-thinking and grunting,
always on the God damned warpath,
always making me ashamed
of my Indian blood.
In nameless American cinemas
our curdling shouts transformed to giggles
which I held in as if an iron lung
were caressing my urge to scream: Yes!
Yes! We gave you corn, but you,
you cornholed us.

III.

Snow sparkles the sootbrick soul of this city.
Part of me wonders if this trip were necessary.
At this graveyard full of dead white men
I feel like the last fly in winter.
Before an ornate grave I cross my standing legs
and pretend to remember
the warmth of my sixteenth winter.
It was then that I decided to leave home
for the first time.
I sat in the outhouse meditating on the *dharma*
of my Indian existence
when all of a sudden a Gutenberg Bible
on the floor mutated
into an outdated Sears and Roebuck catalog

and bore mute testimony
to the power of the written word.
A waning moon illuminated the monastic
silence of the scrawl I sentenced to wall:
Here I sit all broken hearted,
from Indian land I'll soon be parted.

IV.

A something or other fog
dances up against the picture
window of the gin mill where I go
after my gravesite visitation.
I have a shot and a beer chaser and remember
hitching across this country six times in the sixties.
God, how the white highway dashes
integrated the mad
macadam serpent and split my young soul
with envy of his dreams.
God, how stoned by loneliness and lack of food
truckers filed me away as mirage
and zoomed past my hungry mind
fast away into the shaking
legend of American night.

I had no hobo delusions.
The catharsis and sexuality of open roads
was a hope for redemption
unworthy of Green Stamps.
But it's all ancient history.
This surface is bullshit.

Across the street the fog is afraid
of my brand new T-Bird.
One more drink and I head back west.
One more drink in this eastern city.
One more drink to an earth-sleeping poet.
One more drink to Jack
and his beanstalk.

AT THE HOUSE OF GHOSTS

I'm back after twenty years of baiting the trap of the past. This is where I jitterbugged through the sagebrush to be in shape for fall football. Can I still do it? I jog ten yards. The saltgrass tackles me. My legs of iron are gone and my liver aches. Gasping, I stop at an irrigation ditch shrinking in deference to a land-locked seagull above my head. Under the Mason Valley sun, crawdads in the trickle of the ditch fight and flail. Their dancing claws snip bits of sky and lay blankets of shadow on their starving young. A small pool under the bank holds several giant thrashing carp. In a few days their lives will evaporate. I never liked carp, never loved crawdads.

I walk back to the house of ghosts. Here is the airless past that suffocated my youth. The shingles have shied away to show a black tarpaper slip. The remaining window panes have bullet holes in them. No doubt high school kids have partied here. Someone has rammed a car through one wall. In the kitchen sink, a fire has been made from an ancient *National Geographic*. My mother used to subscribe! A page of Himalayan snow is half-burned, browned into another page of Turkish poppies, red as the flame that narrowly missed them. On the floor is a pile of bird bones, feathers spit aside by some marauding cat. Near the avis carcass is a yellowed snapshot. It would be too perfect to say it was an old photo of me. It's some clown I've never seen. He's wearing the letterman's sweater of my old high school and is leaning against a '58 Fairlane with a brown-skinned cheerleader on his arm. He looks as strong as he ever will be. The world awaits him as it once awaited me.

SOMETIMES A WARRIOR COMES TIRED

"When the last red man shall have perished from the earth and his memory among the white men shall have become a myth, these shores shall swarm with the invisible dead of my tribe."   —Chief Seattle

Sometimes a warrior comes tired
in the guise of prepositions
of propositions and says
of thee I sing when he means
what's the use. . .our race is doomed.

And let's face it.
In any waking dream about the most beautiful
Indian girl on Mother Earth I'm going to use
a rubber and blubber about it later
in the memories of nightmares
of the plain wonderful women
I lost at the cost of never being responsible
for something I don't
quite remember now.

Who listens and who cares less
than those gods who dance
with one hand on your ass
and the other pinching their noses
offended by your body stink?

These white men strut into our lives
with invisible robes.
Their imaginary halos encircle our throats
until we look like those African women
in *National Geographic*
with stretched necks.

We like their credo of dominion.
We gratefully accept the results: knives
into our wives, children
dumped along the highway and refrigerators
lined with government cheese.
Yes, we know what is best and stage the old ways
unaware of our blasphemy,
unaware of our Grandfather snickering.

VERDELL REPORTS ON HIS TRIP

"Limited fame gives a lame orgasm, she said and faked
a deep laugh that sent her into a coughing fit. I told her I
was too young to be seduced and allowed how I wouldn't
mind a martini, all the while patting her on the back and
forcing my hand to slide towards her jello behind. I make
extra dry martinis, she said and I noticed she had more
rotten teeth than I did. I sucked my gut into my ribs and
smiled. Ah baby, I thought. You shoulda caught my act
ten years ago. Now I have to fake a hardon just to satisfy
my loneliness for an Indian woman. And no vermouth,
she said. We ended up drinking the cheap vodka with
Tab! I retched so bad I had to go into her bathroom to
calm my bowels and I saw her washed but still stained
panties hanging on the shower curtain. She even had a
book by Vinyl Deloria in a little bamboo magazine rack
next to the toilet. Through the door I heard Neil Young's
After The Goldrush. I knew then that I would marry her.
Move to Chinle and raise sheep, ayyy, *ya ta hey!* And *en-
nut*, she said the next morning. You could, you could. I
told her I would, the next trip to Albuquerque. An angry
Navajo sun was rising and my groin was rubbed red raw."

BURNING TRASH ONE SOBER NIGHT

I. *The Fall From Grace*

A caustic, blinding snow
spewed drunks in clunkers
into deep ditches along both sides
of the death road
to White Clay, Nebraska.

Dancing the ice-reef highway,
I wove through and past
stalled cars to get to the merchants
of death before closing.

Three hours later,
my brain spitting ozone and contempt,
I vowed to quit drinking forever again.
I downed three cups of black coffee
and hauled two bags of newspapers
and stillborn poems to the burn
barrel in the back yard.

Death songs lifted from the fire
and I'm not such a filthy liar I'd say
I heard singers in the crackling flame
if it weren't so horribly true.
Their word shadows droned
into other shadows
and a love fire flamed and gave hope.
Tentacles of light leaped to stinging snow
and sweat dripped down
the rusted barrel.
The fire lived and then died and abrasive
snow scoured my face.
It hurt, but God damn it, it hurt
good like tight pussy.

II. *The Resurrection*

The next day driving through White Clay
listening to "Old Fashioned Revival Time Gospel"
on some Nebraska Panhandle station,
I passed a group of drunken skins
beside their car in the frozen air,
its drive shaft upon the pavement
punctuating an end to their party.

In some static beyond the radio's noise
I heard the song from the night before,
it was clear, it was English and painful:

"Drunken life boils down
to basic commands:

If you tell yourself to quit drinking,
you will.

If you tell yourself you want to die,
you will, my brother, you will."

III. *Ear Wax Once Removed*

Driving the reservation a week later
I saw the white man's green
winter wheat slice up through remnant snows.
An arrogant and sex-starved skunk
driven by early spring weather
danced into the gaping jaws of my T-Bird.
Well-perfumed, I drove in balance,
on the red road toward
the rest of my life.

WAYLON TWO STARS TAKES
HIS SON RABBIT HUNTING

"We had buffalo for food, and their hides for clothing and our tipis. We preferred
hunting to a life of idleness on reservations where we were driven against our will.
We preferred our own way of living. We were no expense to the government then.
All we wanted was peace and to be left alone."   —Crazy Horse

I.

Waylon Two Stars
was born without Magi.
His fifteen year-old

mother hobbled
in slow fearing pain
four sacred times around and
around the government issue
whitewashed shack
in Lakota winter

until the chortling of crows
eating a road-killed rabbit
broke her water.

She went back in
and to her amazement
delivered the brown child herself.

Giddy from pain, she named him
Waylon and then she slept
like the child she was

II.

At forty years of age
Waylon shimmied down winter's road
half-heartedly avoiding turd birds,

little brown fluffs of life
that dive-bombed his car.
In twenty minutes of fast sliding

he had killed a dozen
with little guilt.
Their deaths were almost comforting.

Each small whump sounded like
the cork-string popgun
his mother had given him

at seven when he'd had the mumps.
Microbes had traveled
gland roads from jaw

to groin swelling
his testicles like Christmas oranges
given out by Our Lady

of the Sioux Catholic Church
ten miles from his house near Calico.
His mother, then twenty-two

had made little paper birds
which she had tied with thread
to a dangling light chain.

Waylon shot and shot and with each
hit forgot his hurting
man-sized balls.

III.

Waylon's balls returned to normal
(whatever normal is at the age of seven)
thirteen days later but the weight

of manhood's early imposition then
had cursed him for life, he thought,
glancing at his own son, and driving

from Porcupine to Wounded Knee
through crazed flocks
of brown-feathered *kamikazes*.

He tried not to think of the past
but the more he bit his tongue,
the more unwanted images flew

against his car and into his mind.
A strategic retreat
into the soft sanctity

of childhood was often therapeutic
but when childhood came screaming
for an attention of its own,

it was like a cage full of rabbits
watching their brothers
and sisters being butchered.

IV.

Waylon had known the taste
of rabbits, wild
and tame, and in the tune

of his bounding youth
had seen a mother eat her young
after he had love-cuddled them.

In his teens
he had killed many rabbits
his Grandma raised for eating

and he could not forget
their ball-shriveling screams
at the instant he put the ax

to the soft fur of neck.
He had not eaten rabbit
in twenty years and the taste

was nearly forgotten.
He did recall his mother
rolling the sliced flesh in flour.

Something like chicken,
he would tell any stranger
sauntering through his mind.

You fry them just like chicken.
They go good at picnics
and the last time

he had eaten rabbit was at a picnic
at White Clay Dam
twenty years past

on the week he was scheduled
to depart South Dakota
for the vacuum of Vietnam.

Dusty-faced Indian kids
were running, carrying
cantaloupe, sliced into smiles,

the juice forming tributaries
of temporary sweetness
down their chins toward their hearts.

He sat on the tailgate of an old pickup
talking to his girl,
begging her to release

the lock of thighs
but she never did
and he cursed her

throughout his tour of duty
and never wrote back once
after he shot his first man.

When he did return, he punished
her by placing a ring upon her finger.
And, in a few years, his wife

graced his seed and gave him a son
but the next year she died drunk
when Waylon rolled their car.

V.

Waylon loved his son but felt uneasy
staring into the large brown eyes
of the ten year-old boy.

He couldn't quite figure out the feeling.
It was something like being
caught in a lie.

Part of him was afraid that his son
could see right through him,
past viscera and bone into fear.

Looking at his son, Waylon saw
his own lack of father and he saw
the sins of his mother.

He saw the shame of his race, its hopes
and its nightmares.
He saw himself and was happy, briefly

until he would think of the reason
he was carrying cold steel.
He was taking his son to hunt rabbits

and to stop the furry screaming inside
his skull he reached over
and mussed up his son's hair.

"What's rabbit taste like, Dad?" his smiling
son asked and Waylon shivered and laughed:
"Tastes like chicken."

"Tastes like me," Waylon thought
and wished that his wife
were still living.

PART THREE:

TOMBSTONES

AN INVOICE FOR HER MANY HORSES
ON HIS HILL ABOVE WOUNDED KNEE

for Her Many Horses, Michael

Hoka hey!
Cooking *kabubu* bread
with your commodity
canned stew and meat balls
you offer me some
when I've rolled up dust roads
through the tall pines
through the wildass cows
to get to your house.
Naw, man, I say.
I just need my books back,
those ones you said you'd sell
in Sweden where all you did
was put on war paint
and chase big blonde pussy.

I got 'em here, you say
and you point to a bustle
you're making to sell.
Black and whites, owl dyed orange,
spikes centered with quillwork
by that New Holy woman.
Got to have that, I say.
One circle around the pow-wow arena
they'd carry your corpse back to Nevada,
you say. What do dogeaters know about
anything, I ask and look to the sparse,
ascetic rooms scented with woodsmoke.

That is how a man should live,
I think as I carry my books
to my silver-gray T-Bird
and drive down towards Pine Ridge
not having mentioned the money you owe me.

FIRST DAY OF SPRING SEMESTER

for Joy Harjo

Between classes a white colleague
at the Indian college confides:
"I really got shitfaced last night."
I'm on the wagon but I won't show my hand
and wonder why this guy I hardly know would come
up to me and say this.
I purse my lips and nod my head
not knowing his rhyme or his reason.
What does he want? A fucking medal, or is
he simply baiting me?
I fought long and hard to stay sober last night
and today I'm spellbinding in class.
The Freshman Comp students
are attentive until the break
when the most beautiful young *Lakota* girl
I have even seen
tells me I'm bleeding profusely
from a shaving cut somehow reopened.
Embarrassed by someone so young and beautiful
taking pity on a jaded, fading star
I go telepathic for the remainder of the class
thinking of how in high school I decided to become
a teacher because of the view,
the skirts were so short then,
and I begin bleeding again
not for the pure sake of boredom
but for the beauty of all Indian women.

FRIDAY NIGHT AT WHITE CLAY

Steel scarabs
scurry frantic
at dusk
and reach
critical mass
when they stomp on the gas
like they were studs
and kicking ass
on the toughest dude in town.
But, the truth is, only a few
are strong enough to be human here.

The mushroom's vortex
like a lodestone pulls
us into the ring
vs. singularity.
As tribal people, we are transformed.
When fire and water mix
the people burn
and drown.
We struggle against
no oppression.
We live in a world of denial.
We live in a world of denial.
Our race is puffy, uneducated
and waiting to die,
I tell my old lady
as we drive the three miles
to White Clay, Nebraska
to buy the medicine
of tolerance and bravery.

for Chuck Woodard

A SONG FOR THE SANTEE

On the day after Christmas 1862, 38 Santee Sioux warriors were brought to a specially built gallows and hanged simultaneously. "As the platform fell," reported an eyewitness, "There was one not loud, but prolonged cheer from the soldiery and citizens." The death penalty had been sustained by President Lincoln.

—Benjamin Capps, *The Indians*

Jesus,
my sweet savior Jesus,
I
was a good
brown-skinned
Minnesota
farmer
who wore
a suit
to church.
I
was ready
to take
America
for my wife
until I saw
the false pride
of home hearth
and the dull warmth
of lamplight
when she bent
toward the hanging tree
and made purple
tongued
fruits
of my people.

TEARS OF ONE HUNDRED YEARS:
WOUNDED KNEE, SOUTH DAKOTA 1890-1990

"There was a woman with an infant in her arms who was killed as she almost touched the flag of truce. The women and children were strewn all along the circular village until they were dispatched. Right near the flag of truce, a mother was shot with her infant; the child not knowing that its mother was dead was still nursing. The women, as they were fleeing with their babes were killed together, shot right through, and the women who were heavy with child were also killed. All the Indians fled in three directions, and after most of them had been killed, a cry was made that all those who were not killed or wounded should come forth and they would be safe. Little boys who were not wounded came out of their places of refuge and as soon as they came in sight, a number of soldiers surrounded them and butchered them right there."
—*Chief American Horse* [From a report given to the Commissioner of Indian Affairs in Washington, DC on February 11, 1891.]

Lord Christ of the white church down the road,
my dream
bubble
burst,
rooster raped
by
young drunks burning
black
rubber
on black asphalt
on red
land and
I
was
out of coffee
and
my dogs
had peed
on the rug again
so
I opened a warm can of Bud
and drank a toast to the little boys butchered.

BEFORE SNOW KILLED THE FIRES: A FABLE FOR ST. VALENTINE'S DAY

Jesus gave me a pencil
at the A.A. meeting
and said:
"Lead, head, and hand
make it work,"
before
He inserted
it into my middle-aged heart.

When asked to speak,
I pulled the pencil from my heart
and sketched in blood regrets,
sad valentines for the years
before snow killed the fires
when I loved
wondrous women
in and out
of my life.

After this circus of delirious self-pity
I felt sorry
and sober
and amazingly horny
so I thanked the Lord Jesus
and drove to a bar
full of fire-breath Indian women.

NEVADA RED BLUES

"Where live fire began to inhabit you."   —Pablo Neruda

We live under
slot machine
stars
that jackpot
into the black
velvet
backdrop
and
mirror the greed
of the creatures who soiled our land.

Numa,
it was
not
enough
for
Taibo
to make
our sacred land
a living
though
pustulous
whore.

He
had
to drop
hydrogen bombs
where
thousands
of years
of our blood
spirits lie.

ONE MORNING NEAR LARIMER STREET

An early morning
snowstorming
television
ignites the hotel room
with pallor.
This return to skid row
is my never-ending story.
Her breathing quickens or is it the sound
of the harsh northern wind
nipping at winos
released from the shelters on nearby streets.
I hide my head
between her ample brown breasts.
What are we doing here in Denver?
And if I am atop
a world of flesh,
then why this sad-toned fenestration,
this stumblebum tune
running rampant and skewed
through her tribe and mine?

My cock has chosen to accept
the divine necessity
of *pentimento.*
She is from Fort Hall.
We come from cousin tribes.
We are both far from home-spirit-soil.

SKULDUGGERY

Last winter in Pine Ridge
when the rash of pentagrams and skinned cats
had the old people worried
and the BIA consulted experts on Satanism,
my students asked questions
about witches and their ilk.
"Used to love some a long time ago,"
I said and they laughed.
What I really know of history
is limited by dead brain cells:

His-
story:

The
mask
skull
in
fear
brought
famine
in
witches
by
solemn
Mather
in
Salem,
Mass.

Elementary. . . Like play this poem backwards
for a secret message: The heaviest metal
I know is an aluminum beer can.

SONG OF THE MESSIAH

"The religion started at Walker Lake eighteen years ago is the same that is now agitating the Indian world. There is nothing in it to cause trouble between whites and Indians unless the new Messiah is misquoted and his doctrine misconstrued."
—Frank Campbell [In a letter to the Commissioner of Indian Affairs, November 19, 1890.]

I. *Words Of One Sioux Messenger To Nevada*

Those who know me know
I do not speak out of both
sides of my mouth.
It is you who have sent me
to the land of the Father
to return here and tell what I saw.

When we finally reached His camp,
it was already the moon when the wind
shakes off the leaves and He was not there.
Three days later He returned
and the clear night turned to snow.
The Milky Way
shattered and floated dreaming
down upon leafless sage.
Each star was an ancestor
walking the road
to the spirit world.
Now they were among us
and the Father nodded and smiled.
"Each red spirit now dead
shall return and walk this earth,"
He said in a language
we had never heard
but understood so clearly
that we might have been born
to those rabbit-robed People.
Then, to those of many tribes assembled there,
he uttered more strange words that changed
in mid-air to those of all listeners.

He said, "The white man will vanish
like snowflakes in summer."
He told us to rise.
We did and joined hands.
Slowly we chanted the opening song
shuffling the drag step
until we could shrill:
The Father says so,
The Father says so,
the white men will vanish
the white men will go.

Wovoka said,
"You shall see your Grandfather.
You shall see your grandfathers.
Don't dance with your rifles.
Discard white man silver.
The Father says so,
Wovoka says so!"

II. *Wovoka Sends A Message To A True Believer
Several Years After The Massacre*

I have heard the great sadness
from Wounded Knee.
Some will say the Sioux messengers
weren't listening to me but they were
and in some far away time
what I have said shall come to pass,
the Father says so,
Wovoka says so.
The white man will vanish
like snowflakes in summer.
The earth will open
and swallow them all.
Our mother will belch and be ours once again.

PART FOUR:

COYOTE SONGS

COYOTE NIGHT

A flat tire ten miles
east of Pine Ridge
just past the Wounded Knee turnoff.
I disembark into Siberia
looking for Zhivago.
A non-stopping semi whines away
into a state of exhaustion.
This winter night is held
in silence as if a giant squid
fell upon the land and froze.
Scraggly pines try to feel
up the miserable moon.
Snapping twigs signal
sneaking-up coyotes.
Here there are no distant
garbage trucks,
no all-night neon.
I click the safety off my .22 Llama
and light a cigar.
Coyote eyes float
in deep-ass blackness.
Coyote eyes float
in deep-ass blackness.
Coyote eyes gloat
in black glass glee
and I laugh and return to my car.
It drives pretty good
on three tires.

PYROMANIA

The old lady was late and I
was playing "Blonde on Blonde"
and other ancient anthems
too tired from teaching
to run to the bars
then loin fire came
and the hose was held
until turgid, spewing forth alone
extinguishing with egg-white foam
the napalm flames of empty lust
charred embers sizzling in the dust
and a siren wailing in disgust.
I wish I could say
a Kleenex wiped the molten rust
but the smoke was just too much.

For the first time in a decade
I sampled some herb and then
warbled to the bathroom mirror
to see if I could fashion a Dylan bouffant
from my waist length braided hair.
It was hopeless. Gerbit,
one of my five cats, jumped
into the sink to watch me.
I lit a Marlboro and singed his ear.
I went to bed and dreamed no dreams.
In the morning I awoke to no life.
My eggs were fried solid to torment me.
Bryant Gumbel was whining to Deborah.
Even my car wouldn't start.
I called in sick, poured kerosene
over my legs and ran down the street
begging for a match.
I'll never smoke reefer again, I swear,
the sixties now end in nineteen and ninety.

A FUNERAL PROCESSION OF ONE

Town hopping, shopping,
bored, the old lady
at work, my day off,
I escape the reservation
and fly my T-Bird
between border towns
in Nebraska's Panhandle
where each outskirt
without fail gives the illusion
of white high-rise towers
always transforming
into the constant disappointment
of dirt-hand grain elevators
surrounded by squat lack of vision
and skewed midwestern boredom.
This is the real world of rednecks.
A hard blowing late winter wind
slaps dark clouds
over fields of buzz-cut wheat.
The high harp notes
of an ancient Bob Dylan tape
raped into the cassette deck throttles
the country station newsman
detailing the dead for the day
in the meat packing plants
and for one brief moment
I am glad that America's dying.

SPLENDAIDES

My car dances through morning mist.
The first stop on my red eye
special through Rapid City
is Mister Donut on North St.
My flesh floats onto a plastic seat
and my sight is deaf
to assorted cretins at the counter
except for a dark lady in blue beret
picking her nose at my elbow
and writing something
in a *Big Chief* tablet.

A stolen glance decodes her calligraphy.

Mister Donut
red and pink
stainless steel
Splendaides.

Early morning disdain harbors
the ammonia of recognition.
Does she have my curse? Is
she writing poetry?

In a vortex of invectives
against rhyme and meter,
I curse her and praise myself.
Her fingernails are packed
with earth. Her eyes
are fried eggs with veined embryos.
"Oh boy, Oh boy,"
she whispers aloud.

I look around feigning contempt
and wonder what her scrawl signifies.
Could it be the final message
of Muad'dib?
Splendaides?
Sounds like the international language

of pretense. . .so French.
So *je ne sais quoi.*
It must be holy or a glyph
of madness.
At sanity's behest I deem it best
to ignore the here and now
of her futility.
I crawl inside the *Sioux Falls Argus-Leader.*

Art feature piece:
The influence of Man Ray,
co-father of Dada.

Mister Donut
red and pink
stainless steel
Splendaides

Can this be elegy to Dada?

Maybe, baby.
I wish I could say
but this poor child is only
a puppy dog,
diseased and eating
at the master's table.

She is a humanoid Xerox.
Splendaides
is the brand name of the napkin holder:
a ream of cheap white paper
she scrawls against
her lips and the falling
spittle of her
words.

Splendaides
is the true name of God.

Splendaides is the changeable past
and the code of the unchangeable
future.

Splendaides
is the true God of name.

for Benet Tvedten

DEGREES OF HYDROPHOBIA

"It's the same old story. How can we imagine a new language when the language of the enemy keeps our dismembered tongues tied to its belt?"

—Sherman Alexie

I.

Sunday night blight.
Drunk beyond syntax and losing
metaphors with Liquid Paper
I enter the blasphemy of prayer.
It does no good to burn sage
in my ashtray, scattering faint hope
to the sacred four directions.

I am the untrainable dog that bites
all he sees and stains all the rugs of the world.
I've learned the eternal truths. . . repeatedly
but have forgotten to write them down.
Recurring ghosts refuse to be drowned
by gallons of fiery spirits.
I cannot color the dark at will, so sitting
and shaking I won't question the swill
that my rhyming mentors have taught me
but I know if there is no honor
in a can of spraypaint
there can be no honor in poems.

II.

6:00 p.m. blazing home
from the Indian college, hoping to make
halftime of Monday Night Football
I pop open the lone can of Bud
I've taken as portable relief
from an eight hour siege
of the language of the enemy.
Out of blackness, dumbshit coyote skitters

in front of my T-Bird
carrying a quivering jackrabbit.
The rabbit's eyes glare when I slam
on the brakes and beer goes spraying.
Coyote drops rabbit and each
run away in separate directions.
Coyote is simply a dog without Alpo
I think in the dark with no drink.

III.

Late Monday night drunk and gleeful
the Redskins won, the Redskins won!
My dogs in the yard, happy too
have just scared winos shitless into drunken jogs
that would even make Jesus Christ giggle.
I have good dogs, ball-biters on command,
bed-snugglers late at night.
Most dogs in this town get abandoned
and hang around Sioux Nation Shopping Center
with two-leggeds who were abandoned
as children.
They become kindred spirits
in a land overflowing with ghosts.
Kindred spirits in a dying sun's world.

IV.

Beneath Sirius I dream of ghost dogs
reinventing the bark.
Hounded and clawed by the lost bones
of life, they yip and nip
in folly and foam
at the hovering bitch moon
and its dancing moans of a time long ago
when words had meaning
when language had value
when both men and dogs
were strong silent hunters.

I TRAMP OUT

I tramp out
the ramshackle house
away from the revelry of gestalt
past the barking dogs and dead cars
and slide into my T-Bird
no longer questioning the profound
love that I feel.

I understand the times
and her squat bedroom blossoms
into instant memory
beyond the Pine Ridge
noon-time whistle.

Blurring down the coiled blacktop
like a high school hero
I create *deus ex machina*
from a godless mind.
A chubby little brown puppy
runs under my car
and gives slight rise to my radials.

I stop to inspect the damage
but it's only dust-covered, shivering
and peeing on itself.
When I touch it, it shakes off the dust
and heads down the road
and I do likewise, only slower, slower,
God damn this dying world,
and my endless desire to drink.

AMERICA LOOMED BEFORE US

Lester Hawk dumped a couple hundred pound sacks of corn meal into the trough. I gravied buckets of curdled milk from a fifty gallon drum over it and forty hogs went ape-shit, drooling, farting, scarfing up in minutes the food that the Gods had brought. "What a bunch of pigs," Lester said and then began shouting, "Sooooeeeee, Sooooooooeeeeeee, you capitalist pigs!" The hogs started running in circles, led by one big scroungy monster with gnarled fangs. They wouldn't stop, even after Lester quieted. They were going mad, so we picked up rocks and threw high, hard ones at the leader. Lester beaned him squarely on the right eye. He staggered and toppled to the ground, screaming, thrashing, flipping bits of crushed eye ooze into the sky. Lester got a big boulder and bashed his brains in. Took a buck knife from his Levis and slit open the huge hog stomach. Stinking guts naked onto the thirsty soil. The other hogs, shocked momentarily, soon attacked like piranha. In ten minutes there was nothing left but a pile of gristly bones and hide. We gathered those up and hid them in a gully. The white rancher would never know of our murder, but our childhood had been consumed with the hog flesh. America loomed before us.

THE INTELLECTUAL IN PINE RIDGE

"It was dark and terrible all about me, for all the winds of the world were fighting."
—Black Elk [According to John G. Neihardt]

On the wagon again,
drinking diet Pepsi and potato chips,
typing the channel selector
I fly down Indianapolis Speedway
at 220 miles per hour when I collide
with an overgrown dentist's drill.
I run screaming from his office
but bees of hot lead kiss my body.
I feel the sprinkle of molten spill
from a foundry crucible.
Facedown on a crack dealer's street
I count the machine gun holes
ventilating my soul.

I stagger to my horse and gallop
to the village to warn
the people of charging cavalry
but CNN has beat me there.
I am wheeled into the operating room
to watch a doctor and nurse
shave each other's body hair.
I have won a freezer and a chance
at the mystery prize
but first I must see
which deodorant really works best.

I push the *off* button and sit in the dark
room waiting for Jesus.
My mind is blank. I cannot think.
My finger itches and touches the button.
The tube comes on and I live again!

JOURNAL ENTRY ON THE EVE OF SOBRIETY

1. Got to get up early and dump some baking soda on the
dog spots on the rug & then vacuum. The old lady's hor-
mone anxiety fits might be triggered because the house
smells like a zoo. Might remind her of years we screwed
all night like nuts.

2. Got to buy some cottage cheese, three weeks worth so
I won't look so puffy the next time a mirror sees me. Got
to find a picture of an hibiscus. Just the word opens doors
of delight. A viscous hibiscus? A bisque of Crisco,
hibiscus, and Bisquick? Bred for the floral table? Got to
quit buying these bottles & masturbating with booze-
word ideas.

3. Got to remember when I had fists of steel. Got to go
out tomorrow & challenge the fatherless neighbor boy
who has been triggering my dogs with his b.b. gun. Shit,
he's twenty & has already spent a year enrolled at the
Sioux Falls Pen studying the pipe religion & learning the
whinesongs of the older cons. Damn . . . Got to be adult
& talk calm like a forty-two-year-old college English
teacher. Got to use polysyllabic words to fog his brain
until I can kick his halfbreed balls up to his breathless
throat.

4. Got to remember to be nice to his mother. Got to tell
her to straighten out her son before I become twenty
again & recall the sweet spring grass of baseball season.
Got to tell her I own a *Louisville Slugger* & will homer
his lopsided head. Got to think of something positive
about life on this reservation. Jesus, that's a joke. Got to
go to take a nap now. Christ! This couch of thorns.

GRACE, DIGNITY, AND A SMASHED
HITACHI CLOCK-RADIO ON THE FLOOR

A boudoir Nagasaki
the smashed *Hitachi* clock-radio
on the floor: castrated
components and raped transistors,
digital numbers startled
to the infinite power by whose hand?
This is Monday morning. We have to work!
Christ, I don't remember doing that.
Did you? No, of course not.
We haven't gotten drunk and trashed
the house in some years now.
Look. The pile of junk still sputters
and shakes from impact's instant.
This machine whose sounds we humped to
usually before making coffee
is still buzzing and spurtling the electric
cackle of white light language
from another demented dimension.
Holy bugfuck! Eek and gadzooks.
It sure brings bad memories to bear.

Five years ago we awoke to your car
driven deeply into the corner
of this reservation house.
We barely remembered doing that
but finally recalled the fight we'd had.
After the alarm woke
us that morning and I had blunted
you beyond guilt with foggy thrusting
and the vestigal pain
of my actions could grant no grace,
I had some hair of the dog and explored
the damage to house and ride.

But I don't know how this damn *Hitachi*
got smashed now. We were sober last night.
Have been for a long time.
Maybe our evil doubles did it.
More likely them fucking coyotes.

PART FIVE:

POSTSCRIPTS

A PORTRAIT OF A COUPLE
LIVING ON THE EDGE OF EXISTENCE
ON THE NORTHERN PLAINS

We are mounted against
four off-white walls
yellowed from seven years
of cigarettes, smashed flies, and dead steam
from a Vick's Vaporizer.
You can see us among the eagle wing fans,
the long strands of braided *timpsila,*
the endless school snapshots
of your nieces and nephews
and the nailed up flotsam of varied savage
entities and their imitators.

Four off-white walls
with us mounted upon them.
The windows open
to sub-zero Dakota winter.
Our kitchen shelves overstocked
with hocked commodity foods
from people on liquid diets.
The *Rapid City Journal* folded to an ad
for sunny Majorca.
I close my eyes and hear your lips
feigning kissing my heart.
Outside, in gray vacuumed silence
frozen cottonwoods march four abreast
against the winter in our veins.

Love you? I do!
For Christ's sake, you know that,
but seven years in this federal cage
has rubberized my sword
and made my crusade a cartoon.

TUMBLEWEED SEX PRAYER

On one warm and windy night
driving October plains
half sober between Kadoka and Wanblee
tumbleweeds attacked my T-Bird.
In the midnight dusk of the full moon
legions of tumbleweeds danced down
the hillsides toward the highway
like angry buffalo ghosts.

The king of the tumbleweeds
jumped on the hood of my car
and obscured the fleeting world
underneath my smoking brakes.
Latched on like a brittle, giant octupus,
the mobile skeleton of the thistle
was almost as large as my Ford.
I stopped the car on the lunar plains
and battled the weed until I could anchor it
in a strong gust of wind that jacked it
past the stars
and in that instant my groin grew
granite of its own accord
for the first time in two years
of high blood pressure pills
and I knew that I knew that I knew
. . .Jesus Christ!

74

INTERLUDE: DELMAR FLIES AWAY

In Memory of Delmar "Fudd" Brewer

Standing on the tarmac
at horse pasture Pine Ridge airport
the IHS Cessna twin engine
prop blowback whirlwinds
a vortex of you quarterbacking
Pine Ridge High, blurred images
of your lifelong love affair
with the Beatles, your homers
and championship trophies with
the "Pine Ridge Sioux" softball team
and looking at the myriad tubes
sticking in your arms and face
I feel the three quick punches
that decked me when I made fun
of your brother Dennis' performance
at the "Tough Man Contest" that night
you and I were field testing some Jose Cuervo
and I rub my eyes and see your brothers and sisters,
your nieces and nephews and Josh, Candy,
and Arlene are all crying.
I look at the ground and then at Betty's black shoes
as they move you from the stretcher
to the plane and even though you can't talk,
some tears flow down your face
and I am amazed at the calm silence
as you taxi away, for the last time,
and disappear into Indian clouds.

AT THE BURIAL OF A BALLPLAYER
WHO DIED FROM DIABETES

On a hill
north of Pine Ridge
in furious spring sunlight
under crashing clouds, in face-slapping wind
more than a hundred Sioux are crying.

His heart just gave up fighting
all the pain...
a voice in the group behind me whispers
at the Red Cloud Cemetery.

Shovels are passed from family to friends.
The harsh wind throws covering dirt
in all directions but none of this crowd
is wearing new clothes.
Housed in his shiny new trophy case,
the ballplayer slides home
under sand and clay.
A priest says ashes to dust, other words
I can't hear and in a short, longest while
the grief-filled file towards
their cars and their pickups.

Late that night, somewhere in the black
wind's wail, ancestral spirits wring their hands
their violent tears streak spectral paints
that color me
drunk hours later
in harsh dreams of sorrow
for my wife's little brother.

OWL DREAM SONG:
THE EVE OF DEPARTURE

Exhausted from packing ourselves
into boxes all day
I flop on the couch in a coma.
Now I lay me down to sleep,
tomorrow we move to a white town.

An owl flutters from the dark sockets
of a cottonwood tree and wings
over moonlit fields
and booze-sweltered villages.
It enters my calm mind where
there is no agitated exhortation
of memory's muse
of earthwine traces
of cloned dark faces wearing warpaint
but just the whisper that as Indians
we have failed ourselves.

That old time religion, that urge to drink
begins to rise up from my gut.
O Lord, Lord of the pure green light.
I have seen your rugged crucifix slice
with savage sight, deep the hearts of children,
deep their sad rhymes of night.

Before I know it I am hurtling
down the highway
singing wine songs in a battered car
filled with dead-drunk
and soon-dying warriors.
I feel good and fear the dream's end.

BREAKFAST AT BIG BAT'S CONOCO
CONVENIENCE STORE IN PINE RIDGE

E numu du wi, for all my relations

I.

This town where desire
and defeat share the same
bed and give birth to depravity
is no longer a source of pain to me.
It is the same world I grew up in
and left only to return, forever tethered.
I will not scorn it as a world governed
by grandmothers, welfare, and wine.
It has been my sanctuary.
It has been my home.
This velvet morning I will not deride
the people for practicing
the cardinal virtues of sloth, greed, jealousy,
and drunken gluttony for I
have been the greatest practicioner
of these white world ways.

For now, I will withdraw
across the color line to Rushville, Nebraska,
a small American cowturd town
eighteen miles from Pine Ridge
as the buzzard flies.

II.

In the pastel shades of the dying sun
I drive through ground blizzards
not looking for direction,
nor looking for hope.
I'm past the cheap wine cosmologies
that demand discernment of *Canis Major*
among the equine stars
of many raw mornings.
I'm gone. I'm history.
Never mind that I'll drive
back each day to teach
prevention of run-ons and other such weirdness.
I am leaving the land of the dog eaters.
I will not estimate cans of dogfood
needed for the rest of the winter.
I no longer drink. I no longer can
and will not live in a nation of drunks.
I've trephined the red magnet from my mind
and on this strange and kind morning
the blessing of dead leaves on dead trees
gives but faint clues to hope.
The America I knew went to Hell
with a madman perched in schoolbook storage.
Perhaps all our woes began when we quit
diagramming sentences.
More likely it all began that year I was conceived,
that year we microwaved Japan.

I have no answers and will fight no more.
My life has been spent in cultural dyslexia.
My years are soaked in historical aphasia.
Being a halfbreed is the world's hardest job.
Being sober helps a bit, but I still love
to whine, yes I do.

III.

Big Bat's Conoco Convenience store is open
and I go there for coffee and eggs,
mingling with high school students
and BIA worker drones.
My friend Verdell is there and he tells
me about this *wasicu* woman
who came from the city
to save Indians from themselves.

Verdell speaks:
No doubt she was kinda slobbish
in body and brain.
Why else would an educated white woman
choose to live in a log house
without plumbing?
Choose to be stink?
She used to live with you know who.
When I first met her smell knocked me down.
But you know who. . .
being a broke and horny buck
smiled at her and flexed his thighs.
Jeeza.
Ennut, her hair looked like a house for bugs.
Damn, she was ugly, but damn
she was good.
Her, ennut? You'd never think it, huh?
Had a face like a gang-banged toad.
Had a couple degrees from real good college
back somewhere east.
Who understands these wasicu?
She coulda fucked the brains outa the entire
Iraqi army and saved us a war.
No shit, pard, she was good.
She was the Mother Of All Good Fucking!
It's too bad she killed herself.
It's too bad she ate all those pills.

IV.

This town leads to Hell and back
with occasional intimations of Heaven.
Since I'll no longer live here, I can view
it like an anthropologist.
I can study the shit and smell like Old Spice.
I can teach nouns and verbs
to dimly lit students in dimly lit trailers.
I can be that little train chugging
up the motherfucking hill:
I can do it!
I can do it!

Verdell leaves and I order another egg
with wings of wheat toast on the side.
I remember the Rosicrucian ads
in magazines I read as a kid.
Winged thoughts.
I swallow the egg.
Winged thoughts of the hen.
The world is good.
I'm moving to Rushville, redneck heaven!
Verdell is a liar but I don't care.

It wasn't just that her face was horrendous.
She did have a mind.
Once when I referred to Neihardt's bloodsucking
as *Black Out Speaks*
she actually got huffy.
"Don't you think the Lakota need heros?"
she asked with a grimace
which forced me to pause.
Not if they're invented by white men
I said on a whim and railed
against the fakery of *Dances With Wolves*.
But now it hardly matters.
I'm moving to planet Nebraska
eighteen miles as the snake flies
from here.

V.

Postscript: Sitting Bull speaks
from the pages of a book:
*My friends and relatives. Let us stand
as one family as we did before the white
people led us astray.*

I spend my days sitting in
a little white house
with a white picket fence
built before federal troops came to this town
by train in December of 1890
to march those few miles to Wounded Knee.
I have murdered all inner conflict.
I have no anger, no remorse
and the white world
can just sit on my face
if it wants to.

RED BLUES IN A WHITE TOWN THE DAY
WE BOMB IRAQI WOMEN AND CHILDREN

"Is this Western justice?" Suha al-Turehi asked, pointing to the debris of her single story house. "Is this Western civilization? You are treating us like red Indians."
—Associated Press, February 1991

Sixty degrees, the January thaw
arrives a month late and insidious
sheets of ice in the yard are melting
and flowing into the ancient basement
of my small house in Rushville, Nebraska.
Elated with the warmth of false spring, I walk
upon water with good traction soles,
my push broom shoving ice water
far from the crumbling foundation.
Dayglow clad farm kids from the grammar
school across the ice-packed street look at me
in brief awe as if I were some brand x Jesus
with long hair flowing, carrying no cross
but a push broom.

In a corner of the playground,
three little bright white
wasicu boys are ganging a young Sioux,
chasing him wildly with sharp chunks
of ice picked from the melting earth.
They corner him near the monkey bars
but he escapes in a flailing blur
so they dash back to where he has dropped
his books and jacket and rub muddy ice
on his hand-me-down coat
and slap muddy prints
through the pages of his fifth grade
American history book:
mud fingers on Antietam, on Vietnam,
and a mud hand
on the Washita River.

To my great relief, he begins to battle back.
A small, brown-eyed, raven-haired fury
is unleashed and he counterattacks
the ancestral enemy.
He head-butts and kicks,
knocking the hefty white boys down.
They bleat and run in pained disbelief.
One's nose is bloodied, another's knee is wrenched.
The third grows the heart of a chicken.

My anger dissolves into pride and soothes
something deep in the savage recesses
of my own childhood.
I have known white boys like this.
I have known white towns like this.
I have known the rage to survive.
Years from now these same little white boys
will be in some downtrodden country
planning terror on the computerless
poor of the world or dropping
"smart bombs" on dumb women and children
like they did to Iraqis this week.
Women and children were exploded
by the hundreds as they huddled
seemingly secure in an air raid shelter.
Long distance killers with college degrees
swooped down from heaven
on high tech wings.
They pushed painless buttons
and a sand tribe's blood splashed up
to white clouds
to blue sky
to God's face.

SMALL TOWN NOISE

for Jimmy

It's so peaceful here.
I don't want to burn my neighbor's house
and shoot her family one by one
as they flee from the cleansing flames.
There is no killer bee drone of traffic
late in this medicated night
and no seeking sirens shrieking by
like rapiers of sound
slashing the sensibility of trees
slicing them from root to bough
sending more night bees flying.
There is only a chilled midnight rain
and the moon amid the jigsaw
of black and yellow clouds
in semaphore to a once godless man:
*The true terror of life is that humor
is a tumor and like cancer
is part and parcel of the whole.*

Outside, the silent raindrops tango
and couple in sibilance
with more energy than all the rednecks
in this Nebraska bordertown
fucking at the same instant.
This place is a cosmic yet quiet joke.

We have been here in Rushville for three weeks
and we want to put our car in reverse
and travel the short distance to Pine Ridge.
Verdell once said:
*If an Indian does not live on Indian land
then he is not an Indian.*
And I shit you not, the boy is right.
We're moving back to the reservation
soon when we grow weary of sanity.

NOTES ON THE TEXT

"After Long Silence Marilyn Returns"—*wasicu* (Lakota) white man. *Ennut,* a western Indian affirmation meaning at times: okay, isn't that right, doesn't it, yes, etc. Sometimes spelled *ennit* or *enit*. The term "wannabees" refers to those non-Indians who glorify and covet the Indian way of life, hence want to be Indians. "Squawman" is an historical and contemporary term, usually derogatory, describing white men who marry Indian women.

"A Visit To My Mother's Grave"—The Ghost Dance Prophet Wovoka came to prominence while working in Mason Valley, near the town of Yerington in Northern Nevada. In James Mooney's notes on the Paiute in his book *The Ghost Dance Religion*, he quotes an 1846 report of the Commissioner of Indian Affairs, and concurs that "They are a strong, healthy people. Many of them are employed as laborers on the farms of the white men in all seasons, but they are especially serviceable during the time of harvesting and haymaking." And then, on his own, Mooney adds, "They would be the last Indians in the world to preach a crusade of extermination against the whites, such as the Messiah Religion has been represented to be."

"Among The Dog Eaters"—*kola* (Lakota) friend; *Pejuta Haka* (Lakota) medicine root, the district around the reservation town of Kyle. The term "Dog Eaters" derives from the Sioux custom of eating dogs in ceremonial and other occasions. While this term is usually pejorative if used by a non-Indian, frequently Indians of other tribes refer to the Sioux as "Dog Eaters" with good humor. The varied bands of the Northern Paiute named themselves according to their eating habits. For example, *Cu yui Ticutta*, ancient fish eaters; *Koop Ticutta*, ground squirrel eaters; *Toi Ticutta*, tule eaters, etc.

"Elvis Presley In Pine Ridge"—*Vanilla Ice*, the stage name of a white man who performs and records Black rap music; *wacipi* (Lakota) dance.

"The Hunter's Blood Quickens"—"Slow Elk," an old Indian joke, refers to the cattle of the white ranchers.

"At A Grave In An Eastern City"—The city described here is Lowell, Massachussetts, and the bar is Nicky's. The grave belongs to Jack Kerouac.

"Verdell Reports On His Trip"—*Ya Ta Hey* (Navajo). A common spelling of *Yaa' eh t'ehh*, a greeting, hello, etc. Chinle is a settlement on the Arizona side of the Navajo Reservation.

"Burning Trash One Sober Night"—White Clay, Nebraska, referred to in this and other poems is a small, unincorporated town of approximately twenty residents three miles from Pine Ridge across Nebraska border. Since the reservation is supposedly "dry," the town's annual beer sales nearly equal the two largest cities of Nebraska, Lincoln and Omaha.

"An Invoice For Her Many Horses On His Hill Overlooking Wounded Knee"—*Hoka hey* (Lakota) in varied spellings a greeting, a war cry, or sometimes an interjection meaning something akin to "Welcome!" *Kabubu* (Lakota) pan cooked bread which differs from typical Indian frybread.

"Nevada Red Blues"—*Numa* (Paiute and Comanche) term meaning "The People." This appellation was also used by various other Shoshonean tribes. The word *Taibo* (Paiute) means white man.

"The Song Of The Messiah"—This title is appropriated from John G. Neihardt and a section title of the same name in his book of verse entitled *The Twilight Of The Sioux*. Neihardt, long associated with Nebraska and a self-proclaimed friend of the Indian, is best known for his book *Black Elk Speaks*, which purports to be the words of the Oglala Sioux holy man. One is never quite sure where Neihardt leaves off and Black Elk begins.

"One Morning Near Larimer Street"—Fort Hall, Idaho is the location of the Shoshone-Bannock Reservation. The Bannocks and the Northern Paiutes are related tribes. In the Paiute creation story, *Numanah*, the "Father of all People," or "Creator of all Things," married *Ibidsii*, "Our Mother," and had two boys and two girls. When they grew up, each son married his sister. Then they took to fighting. One family went to Walker Lake in northern Nevada and became the *Agai Ticutta*, the trout eaters. The other family went north and became the *Kotso Ticutta*, the buffalo eaters or the Bannock. After their children left, *Ibidsii* and *Numanah* went up into the sky to live. Considering their children, perhaps this is understandable.

"A Portrait Of A Couple Living On The Edge Of Existence On The Northern Plains"—*Timpsila* (Lakota) wild turnip, often braided and used in a decorative manner, although many Sioux people still add this traditional vegetable to soups.

AFTERWORD
by Tim Giago

In an age when a number of so-called "Native American" writers publishing books would be hard pressed to prove any tribal affiliations, the realistic and powerful writings of Adrian Louis establish him as perhaps the leading *Indian* poet in America. Beyond the critical acclaim he has received, the only way I can describe his style is that it is pure Indian, through and through. His poetry is about Indian life—the good, the bad, and the ugly: lessons in living, to learn from and to share. His thoughts translate into those of a reservation Indian freed from the fog of urbanization. *Among The Dog Eaters* is a remarkable book and I feel the poetry of Adrian Louis is a must for any serious student of Indian literature, but then I am a journalist and not a literary critic. But, as a writer, I often think with my heart and not my mind. This is the Lakota way. As a newspaperman who has spent the past decade covering the Pine Ridge Reservation, I would like to give some background to the people Louis teasingly calls "The Dog Eaters." After all, the land he writes about is my homeland, and the Oglala Sioux are my people.

On the Pine Ridge Reservation, a cut of land one-hundred miles long by fifty miles wide, live nearly 20,000 Lakota people. They are the descendants of Crazy Horse, Red Cloud, Little Wound, Bull Bear, Quiver, Short Bull and other legendary warriors and chiefs of a time not so long ago.

The poverty now is almost overwhelming and hope, at times, seems to be something for other people living in other places, certainly not for the Lakota people of the Pine Ridge Reservation of South Dakota.

For too many years, many of the people searched out ways to escape the poverty and hopelessness. They found temporary respite in cheap wine or cheap drugs. Those who had sunk to the lowest rung of the ladder often lost their minds by sniffing glue, spray paint, and even gasoline fumes. They mixed up and drank a dreadful concoction of Lysol and water. When they could afford it, they immersed their troubles in the sickening, sweet, but intoxicating liquid known throughout the reservation as "green lizard wine."

Some of the locals even refer to Pine Ridge Village, the capital of the reservation, as "Wine Ridge."

But, just when one feels there is no hope, there is no tomorrow, there is no way out, something or someone comes along to dispel these feelings of despair. A teacher (perhaps a traditional holy man), a doctor or nurse, a midwife, a college instructor, a community health worker, a winning basketball team, a report in the local newspaper that things are improving: these are the straws clutched to the bosoms of those who have grown up with fear, without hope, and without dreams.

The powerful poetry of Adrian Louis is in no way intended to make fun of or capitalize on the plight of the Lakota people. After all, he has lived amongst us, eaten frybread with us, sat on the barstool next to us, and laughed and cried with us. His life on the Pine Ridge Reservation has been a roller coaster, to be sure, but not so much different than ours. Our joy has been his joy and our sorrow, his sorrow. He writes about things he has lived, at times through the fog of a mind controlled by a substance earmarked to be his greatest adversary—alcohol. The battle to regain control has been constant, his small victories often followed by gut-wrenching defeats. But then so has this been the lot of many Indian men and women. It is part of the lessons taught in the hard knock schools of survival.

The poems of Adrian Louis often pull their readers, oftentimes kicking and screaming, into the brutal realities of a people struggling to regain control, of a people fighting for their very survival, for their very identity. It is not a pretty picture at times, but neither is life. Not every reader will draw from his poetry these underlying messages that are so often whispered into the ear of the reservation Indian.

Louis, a Northern Paiute, came to the Pine Ridge Reservation on the wings of the great Paiute prophet Wovoka. It was this legendary figure who preached the message brought back to the lands of the Lakota by Short Bull and Kickingbird. It was the message that stirred the people to dancing the *wacipi wanagi*: the Ghost Dance. Sitting Bull fell to the bullets of the tribal police because of this dance, and the followers of Sitanka, Big Foot, died in the biting snow at Wounded Knee on December 29, 1890, directly because of the message carried to the Lakota from Wovoka.

The message of Wovoka was one of hope, one of invincibility, one that promised the return of loved ones who had fallen to the white man's diseases and his bullets. It was a message that promised to end the holocaust of the Lakota people. It was a message that was brutally terminated in the frozen waters and on the icy banks of a creek now known as Wounded Knee.

But the dreams of the Lakota people did not die that day. Perhaps they have been shrouded in uncertainty and despair as the tribe itself emerges from the suffocating grip of two hundred years of colonization. As has occurred in Africa and other countries attempting to throw off the yoke of brutal colonization, the process has been and is a difficult one, the road to recovery long and arduous.

But the fact of the matter is, there is hope. There is a revival of the dream buried underground, secretly kept alive, out of the clutches of the white man, the dream that refused to die.

Oh, it gets lost at times, when the powerful struggle to survive becomes a battle carried on day-to-day, week-to-week, and month-to-month. Survival then becomes the driving force and this primeval instinct has a way of pushing ideologies aside at times, but they remain, ready to be picked up, ready to become a reality.

The poetry of Adrian Louis embraces all these realities. While turning over the rocks to see what emerges, his poetry also surveys the landscape, the blue sky, and the goodness that can be found in man.

The underlying message is—yes—things are bad in the lands he finds himself residing in, but beneath the harshness of life runs a thread of hope.

The poetry of Adrian Louis is a must for all serious students of Indian literature because it grabs the liberal dreamers by the nape of the neck and forces them to look at reality.

In writing about the bitter realities he has lived, perhaps he will exorcise the demons that have torn at his soul and without looking back move on to the next plateau of his life.

—Pine Ridge, South Dakota
January 1992

Authors Notes

Born and raised in Nevada, ADRIAN C. LOUIS is the eldest of twelve children, and is an enrolled member of the Lovelock Paiute Indian Tribe. Louis is a graduate of Brown University where he also earned an M.A. in Creative Writing, and since 1984 has been teaching at Oglala Lakota College on the Pine Ridge Reservation of South Dakota. At different times, he has edited four tribal newspapers, including a stint as Managing Editor of the *Lakota Times*, America's largest Indian newspaper. He was twice nominated as Print Journalist of the Year by the National Indian Media Consortium and was a co-founder of the Native American Press Association.

He has written several books of poems and his work has been widely anthologized. His most recent collection, *Fire Water World* (West End Press: 1989), was the co-winner of Book Award from the Poetry Center at San Francisco State University as the best book of poems published that year. A recipient of fellowships from the Wurlitzer Foundation, the South Dakota Arts Council, the Bush Foundation, and the National Endowment for the Arts, he is currently working on a new collection of poems.

TIM GIAGO is a prominent American Indian journalist. He has been the editor and publisher of the *Lakota Times* newspaper since 1981 as well as a syndicated columnist. An enrolled member of the Oglala Sioux Tribe, he is the recipient of numerous honors including the H.L. Mencken Award. Most recently, he was a Nieman Fellow at Harvard University.

JIMMY SANTIAGO BACA, poet, essayist, and film writer, is a well-known figure in the contemporary Chicano literary movement. He is the author of several books of poetry including *Black Mesa Poems* (New Directions: 1989) and *Immigrants In Our Own Land* (New Directions: 1990).

ALSO AVAILABLE FROM WEST END PRESS

WINNER OF THE 1989 BOOK AWARD FROM THE POETRY CENTER
AT SAN FRANCISCO STATE UNIVERSITY

FIRE WATER WORLD
By ADRIAN C. LOUIS

"*Fire Water World* is a powerful collection of hard-edged poems which refuse to turn away from reality. Although his realism may be hard for some to swallow in comparison to the romantic lyricism of certain contemporary "Indian books," this work establishes Adrian Louis as a major presence in Native American writing. His voice remains distinctly his own—and it is not that of a man who has given up hope. His words sweep away the ashes of the past and clear our vision towards a new dawn."
—JOSEPH BRUCHAC

"*Fire Water World* is a wonderful book, full of fire and loaded up with wonderful poetic surprises. Virtuoso stuff! I'm impressed that the virtuosity never wipes away or disguises the sheer grit and intensity of his work."
—MICHAEL ANANIA

"In *Fire Water World*, Louis has given us one of the angriest, raunchiest books of Native American poetry to be published in a long time. Among the jokes, the drunken brawls, the racist encounters—and deep sadness—Louis emerges as a sharp, visionary poet of great honesty."
—RAY GONZALEZ